ELEVATIONS

THE WEST ELK RANGE | CAPITOL PEAK AND MT. DALY
SNOWMASS, COLORADO

Elevations

POEMS FROM ASPEN AND THE ELK RANGE

PAUL ANDERSEN

ROARING FORK PRESS
BASALT, COLORADO

Elevations
POEMS FROM ASPEN AND THE ELK RANGE

Copyright © 2025 by Paul Andersen

ILLUSTRATIONS | Curt Carpenter

ISBN | 979-8-9892335-4-0

All rights reserved. No part of this book may be reproduced or transmitted in any form or by any means, electronic or mechanical, including photocopying, recording, or by any information storage and retrieval system, without permission in writing from the publisher.

PRINTED IN THE UNITED STATES

ROARING FORK PRESS
Post Office Box 2047 | Basalt, Colorado 81621
andersen@rof.net

TABLE OF CONTENTS

OBSERVATIONS

Aspen Shadows	2
A Doe in the Woods	3
Beautiful Rain	4
Circle Grasses	5
A Covering Blanket	6
Flying with A Raven	7
A Fishing Weasel	8
Fly on the Windowpane	9
Brittany Blue	10
Conejo	11
Beaver Dam	12
The Hot Springs at Christmas	13
My Valley Fills with Snow	14
Early Robin	15
Nightfall at Camp	16
The Moth and the Light	17
The Undying Owl	18
Wild Fire	20
Moonrise	21
Winter Oaks	22
Seen While Bicycle Touring	23
Rain on the Tent	25

PEREGRINATIONS

A Talk in the Woods	28
The One Hundred Giants	29
To John Muir	30
Journey	32
Trout	33
Turkish Moonrise	34
Descent in a Snow Storm	35
If You Dare	36
Henderson Park	37
Josephine Lake	38
Range of Light	39
Schlepping the Pack	40
Kick 'n Glide	41
Alhambra in the Rain	42
The Dying Diva	43
Sierra Day	44
Hungry at High Mountain Lakes	45
Five Feet of Snow	46
Arc of the Trail	48

COGITATIONS

Rachel	50
The Plow Driver	51
To Sing In Spring	52
Rake's Progress	53
Le Bon Docteur	54
Winter Bees	55
Selling Our Old Westy	57
Fur-Bearing Honey	58
Sins of Convenience	59
Striving for Zeros	60
A Symbiosis of Fine Minds	61

RUMINATIONS

He's Her Man	64
Contact!	66
Mystery	67
Cosmic Riddle	68
'Thank You for Your Service'	70
In the Mirror	71
Fifty Years After	72
Bread	73
Work Gloves	74
Campfire	75
Storm Scare	76
Randy's Bear Claw Totem	78
It's All There on the Screen	79
Forgive Us	80
Cigars for Women	81
Of Waste and War	83
Peace in Our Time	84
Autumn Morning	85
Windfall	86
The Old Man	88

REALIZATIONS

Prehensile	90
Another Day	91
What is Love?	92
The One That Got Away	93
Geology	94
Woe Is Me	95
The Libertarian	96
Ode to Sir Walter Raleigh	97
Phallus	99
Weltschmerz	100
The Pitchfork	101

You're In It	102
Pain and Pleasure	103

ABBREVIATIONS

Billy Budd *(by Herman Melville)*	106
War and Peace *(By Leo Tolstoy)*	107
The Visit *(A Play by Friedrich Dürrenmatt)*	109

VOCALIZATIONS

The Downvalley Shuffle	112
Acid Rain	113
Four and Twenty	114
Gary and Donna	115
Ghost Bikers in the Sky	117
Hang Down Your Head, John Ruedi	118
How Do You Solve A Problem Like Gaddafi?	119
Little Hypercar	120
If I Only Had a Job	122
This Land Ain't Your Land	123
Don't Fence Me Out	124
The Leader of Iraq	125
The Night They Tore Down Little Nell	127
Rocky Mountain Buy	129
The Ballad of Tammy and Jimmy	131
The Lost Skiers	132
Avilung	134
Goodwin Greene	135
Downtown	136
The Writer	138

About the Author	141

DEDICATION

This book is dedicated to the poets I most respect—
William Shakespeare, William Wordsworth, Percy Shelley,
John Greenleaf Whittier, Philip Freneau, Henry Longfellow,
Carl Sandburg, Robert Frost, Robert Graves, Sydney Lanier,
Charles Bukowski, Wendell Berry, Mary Oliver,
and many others in whose words I find attunement,
perspective and clarity.

INTRODUCTION

This is my first book of poetry,
a collection that grew over the years from the many and vivid
thoughts and impressions I have been fortunate
to have experienced during four decades
living in the Roaring Fork Valley.

The majority of these poems are traditional and conventional.
They have rhyme and meter.
They are intended to be clear and understandable.
Many are visual. Some are imaginary. Many focus on nature.
Others are philosophical and emotional.

These poems are offered in the spirit
of shared experiences.

OBSERVATIONS

The moon comes glowing like a streetlight,
Its perfect circle crests the ridge.

THE FULL WOLF MOON RISES IN FEBRUARY
ASHCROFT, COLORADO

ASPEN SHADOWS

Their long, straight shadows streak the snow
That blankets the forest floor.
Four feet deep and maybe more,
As winter storms bestow.

I ski among the aspen stands
That bristle white from mountainsides.
My skis break trail, reveal my strides,
On bitter days that chill my hands.

My every gliding stride will bring
Me where the winter sun hits low,
Protracting shadows as winter's slow
Departure makes me long for spring

When stronger light from straight above,
Marks seasons' change, then aspen trees
Sprout catkins with a natural ease
That turn lime green, a shade I love.

I'm here in winter's shadowed world,
All sketched in charcoal, white and black,
In summer, I know I'll be back,
In dappled light with leaves unfurled.

A DOE IN THE WOODS

Leaning with a fluid lunging, walks the silent, stealthy deer.
On pointed hooves she signals worry,
    her ears are perked each sound to hear.
Disinterest I am pretending while watching every subtle motion,
Standing still and not offending, at least that is my gentle notion.

But watch I do across a juniper laid fallen in the quiet wood
Of ages past, its stripped down branches,
    conjuring a somber mood.
The doe and I, the forest beckons, both revelers of solitude.
Each of us take in the other in this communal interlude.

Suddenly, she halts while harking, her pointed ears swivel round.
A neighbor's dog, yipping, barking,
    a toothy cur exhales the sound.
And as the dog runs with yearning, a flash of fur between the trees,
The wary doe coils while turning, and with pounding hooves, she,
    bounding, flees.

BEAUTIFUL RAIN

The falling, dripping, seething, soothing sighing of the rain,
Soft, like a breeze in willows and cool as a dip in a mountain lake.
Caressing as it's falling, easing the world's parched pain.
There are few more comforting sounds at dawn when I awake.

No wind nor gust to stir the weeping clouds as rain they make.
How I love to feel it, touch it, hear it, see it, and, oh, the sweet smell
Of early summer rain when all is verdant, the earth's thirst to slake,
Or, finding that it rained at night and left puddles that will tell

Of rain in a passing, stealthy mist or drumming rhythms on my tin.
How the rain clouds cloak the mountains in a diaphanous cocoon
And gently sweep the ridges with soft billows like a bearded chin
To soak the grass, sparkle on leaves, then drift before the moon.

CIRCLE GRASSES

Circles, some only half,
Are drawn in the sand.
Round and sans serif,
They mark the wind's command.

Still now, as I walk by,
Their dipping quills at rest,
Circles made by stormy skies,
An Aeolian behest.

Nature's neat calligraphy
Upon a canvas small
Is somehow pleasing to the eye,
A delicate, wind-born scrawl.

A COVERING BLANKET

A blanket is cast down from Heaven
And settles on the naked earth.
Six inches deep, or maybe seven,
It gives the world a cushioned berth.

One blessing of this downy quilt
Is how conveniently it covers
All the earth's great sins and guilt
Ethereal as it floats and hovers.

Dirt and garbage, pain and sorrow
Covered up and buried—gone.
Even if it melts tomorrow
The last refrain of a pleasant song.

The quilt drapes down in gentle folds.
On warming earth it forms cascades
That funnel down as earth enfolds
These crystal winter masquerades.

While it's here, it quietly hides
The grimy edge of human life
By rounding shapes and marking strides,
This snowy blanket eases strife.

And when it melts to murky flow,
To brownish lumps of soiled slush,
We see the world that each we know
Lies beneath the snowpack's hush.

FLYING WITH A RAVEN

There's a place I know where I alone go,
A rocky place, a high haven,
Where, in summer's hot sun or winter's cold snow,
There soars a jet black raven.

Like me, it comes here often. With cackling voice,
It rides on the updrafts and breezes.
It dives and soars with the freedom of choice
In summer heat and winter freezes.

I cackle back, and it glances down
At a smallish man, a mere mortal,
Consigned to his realm upon the ground,
Not endowed to soar that portal.

Some envy do I feel, but not chagrin,
For not being able to with raven fly.
For I fly with that bird, again and again,
As it lifts us both into the sky.

A FISHING WEASEL

The rocky, rooted trail follows Maroon Creek as it meanders
Through boulders and fallen trees in whitewater turbulence.
I walked with one eye on the creek for a trout braving the current,
Having seen them struggling upstream with a flash of silver.

Instead, there appeared a long, thin, brown weasel
That hopped from rock to rock along the opposite bank.
The weasel paused atop a granite knob, as if posing for me,
Then into the current it dove and disappeared from sight.

I stopped awestruck in wonder at this brazen immersion.
But nature has its reasons, as I soon realized, because,
In a moment, the weasel appeared downstream and clambered ashore,
Clutching in its jaws a six-inch-long rainbow, madly flapping.

The fish was nearly as long as the weasel, and a fight ensued.
I watched with full attention as the tenacious weasel
Landed the trout and gnawed down for a better purchase.
Then weasel and trout disappeared into the willows.

Long I stood watching for any further drama,
But there was none, aside from the pulsing of the creek.
The trout-fishing weasel should come as no surprise given that
Nature's genius has equipped it with perfect instincts and tools.

As a fisherman, I marvel at that small, feisty predator
Whose success left me nonplussed and a bit envious.
That weasel seemed to want an audience for its aquatic predation,
And I was the fortunate one who happened to serve its purpose.

FLY ON THE WINDOWPANE

Is a fly on the windowpane destined to die
By my hand with the weapon I wield?
With stunning speed its life could yield
No matter how much it may flit and fly.

Buzzing in vain against the pane,
Instinct commands it must get out.
But glass is glass and have no doubt,
Its million wingbeats are all in vain.

Beyond is a world that seems so free,
With blue skies arching over.
Ah, to be a happy free born rover.
Perhaps that's all the fly wants to be.

But the clear hard glass confines, impassable.
To the struggling fly it remains invisible.
There's no passing through the indivisible,
And so the fly becomes irascible.

Battering, battering nonetheless,
In the fly, hope springs eternal.
Life's deepest instincts are internal,
Hence the fly's pitiable duress.

Many a fly is fallen to slaughter,
Dashed against the unforgiving glass.
An insect's fate is a moral morass,
For those who wield the deadly swatter.

BRITTANY BLUE

Blue is a purebred and slightly crazed Brittany,
And I could easily provide you with a litany
Of the times he's simply ignored my call
With his aloof posturing to forestall.

His skinny legs appear so fragile,
But damnation, this dog is incredibly agile.
He'll leap any log, he'll clear any gate,
And when it's dinner time, he's never late.

Such native exuberance man struggles to control,
Whether in the field or on our rug, where he'll roll,
Plastering pesky dog hairs everywhere,
On the bed, on the table, under my favorite chair.

There's no telling what thoughts might play in his head
When asleep, on his back, splayed out in his dog bed,
Where he'll whimper and jerk with spasmodic dreams,
As if chasing a deer, or at least that's how it seems.

But to watch him run is truly a joy.
Not to chase a stick or some plastic throw toy,
But just to run with full speed in any direction,
Despite hip dysplasia, his one imperfection.

If in fate you believe, then know this of Blue:
He's bred to run, no matter what you do.
So watch as he bounds and enjoy it with savor.
Just let Blue run, and do nature a favor.

CONEJO

Two short hops and then a nibble,
Leaf or stem, it doesn't quibble.
Conejo gives its nose a wiggle
Two hops more, it makes us giggle.

BEAVER DAM

Six feet high,
Stacks of willows
Pressed with mud.

Rocks the size
Of grapefruits
On top and wedged.

Water courses
Through and over,
Clear, cold, rushing.

The dam directs
The creek channel
Through willow weir.

Filters the flow,
Slows the water.
A beaver works

To stop the sound
Of running water.
The beaver listens.

THE HOT SPRINGS AT CHRISTMAS

Chlorine fumes and Christmas carols drift on the cold winter air
A small boy runs where he's not supposed to as if he's on a dare.
An old man pads barefoot out the locker room, stiff at the knees.
Sulfurous steam rises in feathery wisps up toward leafless trees.

The old man is steeped in thought, distracted in pursuit
Of foggy notions, not aware he forgot his swimming suit.
A woman watches from the pool in shock and abject terror.
She calls out and waves him back to correct his naked error.

Hot water is piped into the pool from deep underground thermal.
Cellulite and baggy swimsuits reveal aged epidermal.
The heat soothes geriatric folks who soak their aged woes,
And just above the white steam clouds descend the winter snows.

Here was once a sacred spring for Utes and the Shoshone.
They told their warrior stories here, praised a beloved pony.
They came as we for a pleasant soak, a warm and joyful diversion
Among the rock-built pools of old, a comforting immersion.

Leaning back, my legs float up, my head reclines, eyes close.
In liquid words, I'm drifting here with poetry, not prose.
The water rocks me like a cradle, as in a womb I float.
My thoughts are free and flow into every verse I ever wrote.

My vision turns from outside in, I feel mortality,
The failing of the flesh comes due, a harsh reality.
Emissaries from a bygone world are faded now and old
I feel the patter of the snow as winter I behold.

MY VALLEY FILLS WITH SNOW

My valley fills with snow,
Drifting from a cushion cloud.
Moonlight diffuses to a glow,
Dimmed by a diaphanous shroud.

Gradually the storm settles in,
Nudged by a gentle breeze.
Soon the snowfall will begin,
Pattering 'gainst barren trees.

In winter, such has alway been the norm.
I smile when it starts to blow.
A healthy, happy, blustery storm,
A grandiloquent, seasonal show.

EARLY ROBIN

It stands patiently at the edge of the snow
And seems to know not where to go.
All puffed up, its feathery billow
Looking like a fat, downy pillow.

What it eats, I cannot think,
Or how it finds a drop to drink.
For winter cold and snow hold sway,
This robin longs for late spring day.

When listening carefully through its feet
In summer plucks up a worm to eat.
For now a seed or stem must do
Or whatever duff the last wind blew.

"It's only February!" I want to say
And hope the robin flies away
To safer perch and warmer clime,
Not by my window in wintertime.

For seasons must we all obey,
Know when to leave and when to stay.
To thrive, we must respect the date,
Don't come early and never come late.

NIGHTFALL AT CAMP

Night comes in, and the breeze ceases.
Only quiet and darkness know the woods.
Our voices drop to mere whispers.

The zipper of a tent is deafening.
The rustle of my sleeping bag,
Every sound is an interruption.

Good dreams to you, my friend,
And good night, world.
One more glance at the heavens.

The bashful moon
Peaks through the clouds,
And all is still.

THE MOTH AND THE LIGHT

In my big, overstuffed chair
I cock the reading lamp just right.
With book in hand, no other care,
I read in perfect light.

The words compress into a story.
With characters, the plot unfolds.
A hero's journey, the path to glory.
A brave man who breaks the molds.

That's when the moth flits into view,
Darting to the lamp so bright.
I start, there's nothing else to do
When on my page it comes to lite.

Most might simply shut the book,
Make the moth a dusty smudge.
But upon it kindly I must look.
I bear that tiny life no grudge.

The moth is drawn to light and heat.
I submit to its machinations.
I damp the light, prop up my feet.
I'm in no mood for confrontations

THE UNDYING OWL

In the thin, cold light of a wintry day,
On a hedge of green an owlette lay,
Damaged by unseen collision,
The owl met glass with grim precision.

Our triple windows hold in the heat,
An invisible wall for wings that beat.
A heartfelt thud, the diabolical pane
Left owlette stunned in mortal pain.

Flung down on earth, this perch its last.
I saw it there during noon repast.
Stunned from glassy, hard reflection
In winter light, a fatal deception.

At night it soared from snow-decked trees
To take a rabbit, as it pleased,
Which feeds on greenery outside
Where rabbits contentedly abide.

Sadly, watch I, the still small bird.
To my wife, I said not one word,
For she would weep to feel the loss
Of an owlette's pain from glassy gloss.

The feathered head all nodded o'er,
A crumpled wing right by my door.
Eyes faintly blink as resilience brings
Back to life, this predator with wings.

Not dead! Not dead! The owl revives.
Its life pulse quickens, its will survives.
The round head swivels to my eager gaze.
I watch with hope, my hope is raised.

Our eyes meet in unblinking stare.
Mine pale blue, its yellow with dare.
Side to side I move my head.
It tracks my motion, the owl's not dead.

I raise both open hands to shy it.
Eyes widen, wings gather to fly. It
Launches from its evergreen blind
And flits away, new prey to find.

Away from windows of my house,
The owlette hunts a winter mouse,
Or, with its predatory habit,
Perhaps a plump and furry rabbit.

I won't forget its pinpoint gaze,
Unfettered counting out its days.
A free flown being that once touched down,
A feathery visitor without a sound.

WILD FIRE

Plume of soot-tinged cloud arising.
Tongues of white hot flames comprising.
A voice of deepest animal roar,
Burning, churning, burning more.
Forest spurning all that flees,
Running from the hot disease.
Come the winds that know no quarter,
Blasting like an open forge.
The fire rises higher, higher
Green forest becomes a flaming pyre.
The once lush mountain,
Pulsing like a red hot fountain,
Malevolence in its heated breath.
Above it a thick pall of death.
Watch it fester, hear it feast,
Booming when the trees and all
Enflame with crackling tinder.
A fearsome sight that does enthrall.
Spewing fire and clouds of smoke.
Alive, it soars on orange wings
Swooping down on living things.

MOONRISE

The moon comes glowing silver bright,
Its perfect circle crests the ridge.
Reflecting sun in startling white,
From day to night, it forms a bridge.

Silent comes the rising moontide,
Potent force of gravity's pull.
I watch it from my downy bedside.
It stares back at me, round and full.

If once a year, this brilliant disk,
Did rise and shine for us to see,
We'd stop and stare, ignore the risk
That putting lives on hold can be.

We find our gaze is upward raised.
Mundane affairs seem plain and dull.
We're altered, mesmerized and dazed.
The moonlight beams down thoughts to mull.

WINTER OAKS

Rough arms entwine the gnarled woods,
Barring entry, stout forest guards.
Acorns offer squirrels their goods,
Their sweetness with age retards.

Now the oaks' sweet fruit is gone.
From squirrels there's nary a chatter.
The winter has settled snow upon
And covered all with crystal matter.

Whiter than the frothing creek foam
The snow mantles twisting limbs.
Winter oaks provide a sacred home,
A chapel right for woodland hymns.

Arched and winding branches hold
The snow in just the way it fell.
On a windless night of bitter cold,
Sifting down in nature's spell.

The gnarled oaks, without complaint,
Display their soft and gauzy load,
Accepting the burden without restraint
Along the lightly traveled road.

SEEN WHILE BICYCLE TOURING

Snakes and birds and bats and things,
Squished upon the road.
Anything with legs or wings,
Squished upon the road.

Cars and trucks and tourist buses
Leave behind a trail of smusses.
Robins and wrens and even thrushes,
Squished upon the road.

Pedal by, you're feeling mellow,
There you see a toad.
How it's insides look like Jell-O,
Squished upon the road.

Scaly snakes you once decried 'em,
Now you see the stuff inside 'em,
Wish someone would quickly hide 'em,
Squished upon the road.

See the hedgehog, nicely flattened,
Squished upon the road.
Now you see on what he's fattened,
Squished upon the road.

Never had a chance to scurry,
Feathered fowl or something furry,
Wiped out in a blinding fury and
Squished upon the road.

See that critter, lost its head,
Squished upon the road.
Just a tiny smudge of red,
Squished upon the road.

See the rat it's really writhing,
Due to someone's careless driving.
Nothing can be long surviving
Squished upon the road.

I saw something strange today,
Squished upon the road.
What it was, I couldn't say,
Squished upon the road.

No remorse, no funeral pyre
When the elk and deer expire,
Crushed beneath a radial tire
And squished upon the road.

They meet their grizzly fates at night,
Squished upon the road.
Blinded in a bright headlight and
Squished upon the road.

So the next time you're out biking
You may see things you're not liking.
While you slept, the cars were striking
Things upon the road.

RAIN ON THE TENT

The pianissimo of gentle rain
Stirs me from my sleep, awake.
The sound alarms my wakeful brain.
What are the measures I must take?

My pack, my food, my camping gear,
I run through the familiar list.
Wetness is a primal fear.
Will it pour or shortly desist?

Now come heavier drops, staccato on the fly.
The rain is falling all around.
Assured, I know I'm warm and dry.
I know my gear is safe and sound.

A flash of lightning strobes the night.
I snuggle deeper into my cocoon.
Thunder crashes with rumbling might,
And later comes the dim, round moon.

PEREGRINATIONS

Back and forth, forth and back,
All along the woodland track.

TAGERT HUT | ALFRED A. BRAUN HUT SYSTEM
ASHCROFT, COLORADO

A TALK IN THE WOODS

I walk this mountain trail alone,
With no companions to speak.
I walk alone to roam and atone
And to be by myself at the creek.

Here I find a friend to converse
On any topic I have in mind.
The voice of the water is never adverse,
But seems invariably kind.

Onward into the forest I find
The breeze in the trees is my friend.
The voice of the wind is there to remind
That one day my trail will end.

And when it does, I'll have had a good walk,
With loneliness never a sorrow.
For with all of nature I've had a good talk,
And hope for another tomorrow.

THE ONE HUNDRED GIANTS

Giants tower, living cathedrals, rooted in the sod,
Joyce Kilmer's poetic paean: trees are made by God.
They rise from the graves of those come before
Whose long, round bodies decay on the forest floor.
Overwhelmed with awe and deep admiration,
I give praise for sequoia salvation.

TO JOHN MUIR

In walking the trails, I think of John Muir,
That pioneering Druid who scaled nameless peaks
And described his climbs with words so fluid,
The poetry of inspiration.

He sought the high peaks of the Sierras,
Long rambles in the sacred Range of Light.
So called for their bright granite facets,
The sunshine's blinding, daytime sight.

Muir said that when he ventured out
He learned that he was going in.
The mountains became his church primeval,
Which he took for his wedded bride.

Oh, that we, one and all, may find
Such heartfelt passion in a beloved,
Like young, ardent, loving courtiers
Seeking favors from the very fairest.

Beauty lies in the earth's lush fabric,
Where swarms of flies flit the sunlit shafts,
That filter through the primal forest
Where teeming life thrives extant.

Muir's sacred grove is a ring of Sequoia
Forming a veritable cathedral apex,
A wooded, living, natural chancellery,
A place where Moses would have worshipped.

I sit quietly in the center, feeling grateful,
For the love and fellowship I feel for the man,
For which is named this woodland sanctuary,
This holy concentricity.

Gazing up to where the topmost branches
Interlock their limbs in a holy union,
I know intuitively that far below me
Their hidden roots complete the sacred circle.

A cool breeze wafts around me,
As do the songs of birds now singing.
Giving prayer in a still and somber forest,
Reverent for he whose name adorns it.

JOURNEY

The first step begins it,
The last step ends it.
All steps between are what make the journey.
Beginning and ending are only points.
The journey is the continuum that gives them meaning.
Beginning is in the past.
Ending is in the future.
Journeying is the now that takes us from and gets us to.

TROUT

A speckled trout
With blood red gills
Looks up at me
Amid our struggle.

I look guiltily down
Through clear ripples
Of the high, deep lake
Near the top of the pass.

The speckled trout
With blood red gills
Fills the frying pan
Edge to edge with sizzles.

Cooking over the crackling fire,
Hissing hot with butter drizzled,
A perfume rises, crisp and salty.
My stomach rumbles with demand.

The meat is tender, pink and flaky
Hair-like bones strewn on my plate
Are washed off in the same lake
From where the fresh trout dinner came.

TURKISH MOONRISE

A crescent moon, piercing, rises,
A sideways smile, the cosmic grin.
Silver shines the sharpened ends
As on the Turkish flag, with star.

I saw that flag against blue sky,
Red, it fluttered madly then.
Ferrying from Rhodes to Fethiye
Where tombs are carved in cliff faces.

Merhaba! They sing out hello
With a warm and pleasant greeting
To moon-beamed travelers on a lark
In a moment fleeting.

DESCENT IN A SNOW STORM

He clicks his heavy boots into bindings
And glides off down the steepening hill.
The snow is white, the wind is blinding,
His tracks they soon with powder fill.

Behind him lingers in his wake
A pluming cloud of cold, white smoke.
The airborne crystals shatter, break
The hush that Old Man Winter spoke.

The atmosphere is white and bitter.
He feels the brush and burn of frost.
As snowflakes patter down like litter,
The refuse angels carelessly toss.

The mountain furnishes the snow show
In a setting bright with romance.
Gravity his partner in a ballroom of snow.
He soars in this his Alpine dance.

IF YOU DARE

Daring is what often counts.
This is why the pressure mounts.
Daring is to seek and strive
For what it means to be alive.

Dare to seek the truth steadfast,
Released from bondage of the past.
To be just who you want to be.
With liberty, unfettered, free,

Setting sail to find your peace
Into a storm without surcease.
You list to starboard, then to port
As seagulls cry a shrill retort.

Like Odysseus lashed onto the mast,
With ropes and chains to hold him fast,
While sirens called with fraught temptation
On this his homeward bound gyration.

The land is near, you'll soon be there
To breathe the flower-scented air.
Nature's sweet and rich perfume,
The scent of love, the reek of doom.

With fate you travel, hand-in-hand
As wooden bow nudges onto sand.
You're safe on this, the distant shore,
Where calamity will reign no more.

So, now you're here, what's next in store?
To live without a care?
To ask of life just one thing more:
A world of wonder, if you dare.

HENDERSON PARK

Narrow opening in the dark timber,
Light of day!
Tawny meadow where you breathe
Fragrant mountain air
Wafted on a fresh morning breeze.
Eyes search for elk and deer,
Bear, maybe a moose.
This is their home, more likely seen at night
When the owl calls
And the trees creak
With the rush of wind
And the clouds sweep overhead
Misting a rising moon.
Then you might see them
With your night eyes
Dilated wide to probe the dark.
You've come to a place where nature abides,
At my pagan church at Henderson Park.

JOSEPHINE LAKE

Too small for most,
Overlooked, unknown
In the vastness of the wilderness.

Josephine Lake gathers waters
From the snow as it melts slowly
From a steep, north-facing cirque,

Tumbled boulders wall up one side.
On the other shore, a lateral moraine.
Lake and timber make for good camping.

Bright orange fireweed
Grows at the lake edge
With small, upstart spruce.

Tiny fingerlings hit the surface
And take flies hard, with a gulp.
They flash away if your shadow crosses.

A bird chirps.
A mosquito whines.
Cutthroats swirl the water.

Small, gentle splashes
On a still day leave ripples
That spread over the calm surface.

A pall of smoke
Dims the mountain peaks
From nearby forest blazes.

I settle on my sleeping pad
To take a long, deserved rest.
My pack was heavy today.

RANGE OF LIGHT

Granite radiance electrifies the air,
Spreading sun's rays with luminous glow.
Lakes glitter with ripples fair,
Multifaceted in silvery show.

Nature's beauty inspires awe,
Touching deep our human core.
Beauty sublime in wilderness raw,
Made known in tales and lore.

Our senses perceive something divine,
Channeling our distant past.
We know it as something undefined,
But with reverence we firmly grasp.

Creation is life, what some call God,
All from the same, unknowable source.
Malleable clay, the impressionable clod,
Traveling upon an unknown course.

SCHLEPPING THE PACK

It holds me in 60 liters,
All I need, but not all I want:
Cold beer, a hot bath at night.

I heft it onto one knee,
Then swing it up to my shoulder.
Its weight is my mobile home.

I strap it tightly around my waist,
Feel it pull me backwards,
Forcing me to lean it forward.

Imbalance causes a slight totter,
Shifting feet, adjusting straps
To walk the mountain trails.

Rocks as the glaciers left them,
Roots as the trees grow them.
They make my every step uneven.

Here's camp, but make sure
Before dropping the pack,
It's the place I want to stay.

Once it hits the ground, I
Won't pick it up until morning,
When I will bear it another day.

KICK 'N GLIDE

Kick 'n glide, kick 'n glide.
That's the way to make them slide.
Channeled in the dual grooves,
Feeling how my body moves.

Back and forth, forth and back,
All along the woodland track.
Blue or green, the wax I pick
Gives my skis the proper kick.

Up the hill, then down I go
On the gliding, slipping snow.
Feel the rhythm, left then right,
Bluebird sky or moonlit night.

ALHAMBRA IN THE RAIN

Morning brings to old Grenada the hiss of falling rain.
On the cobbled street outside our room, it gurgles into a square stone drain.
Rain, some linguists say, falls mainly on the plain.
In this hilly cityscape, it falls and falls again.

The line is short, we pay our fare, we're ushered through the gate,
A vast stone arch expertly built by Moorish caliphate.
Umbrellas furled we stroll into a courtyard so ornate
To stare at a reflecting pool that raindrops perforate.

Complex and wondrous architecture, stonework that's divine.
The hands that formed this palatial grandeur, their craft did refine.
The men who toiled, who built this hall, with stone their lives combine.
Their unsurpassed craftsmanship, we see it as a sign.

Enslaved to labor mightily, no invoice and no bid,
Their blood spent on the chiseled stone we're wandering amid.
The whip, the prod, the threat of death, when done they were got rid.
Their lives were tossed, their labors lost, from Mecca to Madrid.

In sheets of rain the gutters flow, the stone is washed clean.
This palace bears the mournful cries of human suffering.
We touch the satin columns, all polished to a sheen.
The hands that built this palace were as ours, but now unseen.

We think we know the beauty here within this elegant scene.
We recognize the sacrifices time cannot redeem.
We measure brutal history as cruelty obscene.
Imagining the great travails etched on this timeworn screen.

But we cannot conceive how deep the sting of human pain,
Of slaves who built the ancient world in the heart of Spain.
A deluge cloaks the rich facades of loss for some, our gain.
We splash through puddles, cameras poised, amid the falling rain.

THE DYING DIVA

She was thin, delicate, fragile, a faded beauty.
A bright aura shone as she smiled through her pain.
Sitting up in bed, she beckoned to her husband, whose duty
Was to bring me to her, and for him not to remain.

I tentatively approached, past the attending maid.
I sat on her bedside, where she reclined in a gown of white.
Her hair was made perfect, twisted in a thick braid.
Her cheeks were rouged, and her eyes were clear and bright.

She self-consciously offered me her vein-crossed hand.
I held it like a delicate, perishing flower.
She said that as a prima ballerina, she had danced in a far off land.
Her subtle perfume conveyed a sweet, exotic garden bower.

I felt like I was in the presence of a regal, fabled queen,
A noble woman of consummate composure and tender grace.
Her inner nature was elevated and, oh, so serene.
Her lost beauty shone in the lines of her resigned and stricken face.

SIERRA DAY

Light snow patters on my tent
Campsite thirteen dollars rent.
The creekside setting heaven-sent.
Piling up, Sierra cement.

In the morning, with packs cinched tight,
We set off in the bright sunlight.
Uphill with the switchbacks tight,
Granite peaks gleam blinding bright.

Sequoia, redwood, sugar pine,
Towering, massive, rise sublime,
Touch with awe this heart of mine
On a trail to the divine.

HUNGRY AT HIGH MOUNTAIN LAKES

At the first lake, we could have thrived;
Caught enough fish to survive.
Two pan-size cutthroats nearly made a dinner.
We ate greedily, but still felt thinner.

The second lake had bigger trout,
But damned if we could pull one out.
Beneath the ripples they sniffed our flies,
But they wouldn't bite, despite our tries.

We threw in everything, even a grasshopper
Expertly hooked and floated with a bobber,
We tried a hairy lure with several hidden hooks,
Dangerous to handle and very strange in looks.

Next was an exotic fly that could have been endearing
As a Christmas ornament or perhaps an earring.
We tried a fancy Mepps, a spinner made in France,
But nothing would these fattened trout entrance.

The third lake, shallow, had been winter killed,
A tarn imprinted with elk tracks in the till.
On a three-day camping trip, depending on fish,
We'd be cannibals with an unappealing dish.

FIVE FEET OF SNOW

Levitating without a sound
Over five feet of Colorado snow,
Floating over solid ground,
The snowy depths unplumbed below.

Where voles and moles might feel our treads
In the blackness of their cozy caves,
Snuggled warm in grassy beds,
Their somnambulistic graves.

Our skis skim across the depths below,
Oblivious to all that's under.
Bridging thus the layered snow
That provides us skiers wonder.

Five feet of snow our weight can bear,
Accumulated high up in the range.
Three hours skinning took us there.
Levitation feels quite strange.

Before us spreads the vast untrod,
A bright, white snowpack formation,
I'm feeling like a Nordic god,
King Odin's reincarnation.

Deep snow like this not seen in years
In bitter January's mid.
The trail we hike in summertime
Lies beneath us and well hid.

Stand atop the virgin glisten,
High above the solid ground,
We pause a moment, stop and listen;
The snow absorbs all human sound.

Above us swirl the icy clouds,
Below us chimes hoarfrosted snow.
The trees are flocked with cotton shrouds,
A sight of winter few can know.

ARC OF THE TRAIL

Up the hill it climbs,
A faint pathway etched.
Inviting in such desert climes
Where imagination is stretched.

A side canyon beckons here,
In gentle curve, the trail
Arcs faintly and unclear
Like a siding's rusted rail.

The true seeker must explore
Each alluring faint defile,
Not leave it for another day,
But walk today the extra mile.

COGITATIONS

Yet those who, feckless, acquire more zeros
Are widely revered as cultural heroes.

GRUMMAN GULFSTREAMS AT THE PITKIN COUNTY AIRPORT
ASPEN, COLORADO

RACHEL

Behind the US Postal counter she marks her time and works,
Servicing mail for friendly folks, and occasional jerks.
She smiles hello, winks, her short-bobbed hair is reddish.
It sprouts garishly from her head like a kind of fetish.

She weighs boxes, stamps postmarks, handles envelopes.
Eight hours, six days a week, does she have other hopes?
Time for rest, time for fun, a respite on the weekends?
Not when job number two intervenes to meet her meek ends.

At the convenience store on Sunday, chipping sidewalk ice,
Her red head down, her arms at work, and no more making nice.
Why must Rachel labor so hard, like so many others?
Pay off the card, her daughter's school, support one of her brothers?

Home at last, she's on the couch, the TV comes to life.
At last the world can go to Hell, she's done, and no man's wife.
The news comes on, a Texas school, there's been a shooting spree.
She notes the toll, sixteen are dead. "There's folks worse off than me."

THE PLOW DRIVER

The blade rattles and clanks on the ice below the snow,
Pushing a wave of powdery fluff in four-wheel-drive low.
The plow driver, cigarette clamped between pressed lips
Enjoys a tumbler of rum and Coke, from which he sips.

He likes it best at night, plowing in bright headlights.
Snowflakes tumble into the beams, at which he delights.
He's out of the house where the wife watches her show.
Enjoys the power of the Jeep while pushing snow.

His pathway is clear, now he works up the banks.
There's no one to see him, no one to give thanks.
But he's never lonely, in the fury of the storm,
He does it his way, with no need to conform.

A push against the snow, moving it this way and that,
Answering the call whether winter's lean or fat.
One day he won't be here, he hears himself say,
Then some other plowboy can make his own way.

He thinks he'll be remembered for his touch on the plow.
Anyone who's plowed a road will know that he knew how.
Only springtime will erase the wide swaths he made
Roaring down the lower flats, chained up for the steep grade.

He feels good about his nocturnal labors,
Knowing the drivers appreciate his favors.
It's no wonder the plowman loves his career.
He toggles down the blade and shoves it in gear.

TO SING IN SPRING

Springtime birdsong, pure and brilliant,
Sang the warbler I heard at dawn.
The soul of nature is fresh, resilient
On the wobbling legs of the newborn fawn.

Sensing underground, the waking worms,
Standing still, the hungry, eager robin,
Pecking at the one that noticeably squirms.
Down the hatch, with his red head bobbin.'

The bluebird perches when it's chill.
Ruffled feathers are puffed up and fat.
It must work hard to get its fill.
Snaps up a fly, or perhaps a gnat.

Airborne lizards, blessed with wings,
Evolution's feathered air force.
Happy every day it sings
Songs direct from nature's source.

To sing in spring, we each must bring
A harmonic chorus to all creation.
A song for spring; let's all now sing
And honor our sacred habitation.

RAKE'S PROGRESS

With the sweep of leaves before my rake
On a cool, blue autumn day,
I pause and for a moment make
The time to stand in a sunlit ray.

How like the many worldly woes
Are leaves that cartwheel down.
In autumn, not long before the snows
And winter's pure white gown.

My rake sweeps clean the still green grass,
Now free of yellowed leaves.
I gather piles and yet, alas,
I feel a spirit grieves.

My leafy pile grows by every sweep.
Rake's progress shows my labor.
But there are trees, their leaves still keep,
The trees of my closest neighbor.

Just as I make the final pull,
The crunchy leaves to gather,
There comes a wind from out the lull
And showers of leaves do scatter.

Could the world be swept and guided
By a divine, beneficial rake,
Then peace and love could be abided.
This hopeful wish I make.

Thinking how mankind has bled
With trauma, strife and grief.
There are trees still left unshed,
And so I turn another leaf.

LE BON DOCTEUR

To the service of others, Albert Schweitzer gave his life.
Surrendered his music and scholasticism to a purpose higher.
He left Europe for Africa, supported by his trusting wife
And plunged himself into medicine with a purifying fire.

He was deemed a pure soul, without sin or mortal taint.
There was no one else living who modeled such grace.
A lofty sobriquet, he was dubbed, "The Living Saint."
A conceit the self-effacing doctor wished he could erase.

"He's not a saint," admonished a dear, old friend.
"After all, Albert Schweitzer was but a man."
Which made him all the more remarkable to lend
His skill, his care so that others could withstand

The suffering of life's unkindness and despair,
Fellow travelers on this whirling sphere of earth,
Who found themselves nurtured by the good doctor's care
On the path to death from the door of birth.

In Aspen, Le bon Docteur invoked Goethe's honored spirit.
With humility, he raised the bar on errant human nature.
In the Saarinen tent, speaking French, so the world could hear it,
Transcendence was key to his spiritual nomenclature.

At Paepcke Park stands the weathered bronze bust
Beneath the tall, sheltering boughs of needled spruce.
The marble block reminds us of ashes and dust
And in our spiritual lives to be of good use.

WINTER BEES

They got into the house in a firewood log,
Holed up in a fast frozen hive.
Set by the stove near the sleeping dog
Where the heat of the stove would revive.

The man of the house stacked the fateful load
Before his night's respite to take.
Drying wood overnight was his woodsman's code
As the fire next morning was easier to make.

The icy log soon began to melt
In the glow of the stove so warm,
And the wakening bees began to stir,
And they spewed from the log in a swarm.

All through the house came a buzzing vibration
While the man and the wife were in bed.
No one was aware of the situation,
Nor harbored a sense of dread.

The dog was the first one to realize
That winter bees know how to sting.
The couple in bed heard its painful cries
From the pain that the stings did bring.

The man jumped up and out of bed
To see why old 'Laddie' was yelping.
He ran downstairs and got stung on the head
And the curses he shouted weren't helping.

The wife jumped up to offer her help,
To see why dog and man were frantic.
The man was swatting, the dog did yelp.
To the wife, it all seemed like some antic.

Until one errant bee went right to its mark
And stung her square on the nose.
The scream that she issued echoed in the dark
And interrupted the neighbors' repose.

Doors were flung open, windows pushed wide
With brooms the man and wife fought back
From the house all the bees were shied
All the wood was returned to the stack.

The community heard how the dormant bees
Displaced the couple that night.
They were stung on heads, on hands, on knees,
And the story was told with delight.

SELLING OUR OLD WESTY

"My, she was yar . . . ," said my son of our camper.
Quoting a line from "The Philadelphia Story,"
Spoken of a yacht that was Dexter's true glory.

When our Westy just purred, its faults we demurred.
Her mileage was high, her vintage was old.
So, asking twelve grand was shamefully bold.

We priced high the old thing, despite foibles and quirks:
The slow battery drain and the clutch chatter jerks. P
erhaps we didn't really want to sell it.

We found the right buyer to make this adoption,
A soulful young gal, who offered an option:
"Knock off two grand, I'll pay you ten thousand."

But we held out for more, until an old Westy owner
Had just one look, and our searching was over.
So we gave him the title, we unscrewed the plates,

His check turned out good; we were done with our dealings.
He drove it away and we watched with mixed feelings.
We said quick good-byes, consigned them to their fates.

The money would never make up for our parting,
For the Westy we loved, even some days not starting.
To the new owner, we wished "best of luck!"

FUR-BEARING HONEY

She's a fur-bearing honey
Wears a coat that's worth more money
Than she ever earned in her life.
She's got cape that's chinchilla,
Goes with shoes of Armadillo.
She's a big executive's wife.

On city streets she goes walkin',
And she hears people talkin',
It's her beaver that they adore.
Cause she's a fur-bearing baby,
Never had a case of rabies,
And she's headin' to the furrier store.

Now people think she's callused
Cause she's wearin' a fox,
Hangin' right down to her knees.
But they're just hypocrites for
Wearin' woolen ski socks.
Imagine how those sheep
They must freeze.

Well she's a fur-bearing Mabel,
From her mink to her sable,
Keeps her warm, if she goes outside.
Her clothes are sure dapper,
Cause she gets 'em from a trapper.
It's just an animal's hide.

You know that she nearly fainted
When her ermine was spray painted,
It was new, right out of the box.
Cause she's a fur-bearing Betty
From the Serengeti,
She's a twentieth century fox.

SINS OF CONVENIENCE

Benjamin Franklin owned slaves who toiled for his ease,
An Enlightenment thinker who used humans to please.
He denied moral failings while co-founding a nation.
Became an abolitionist only to stop immigration.
Knew ownership of fellow man was a convenient sin
As the creep of moral wrong crawled under his skin.

So with Native Americans, victims of genocide.
So with poisoning water with toxic pesticide.
So with burning dirty coal to fuel dirty industries,
Convenient sins to enrich capitalist ministries.
Exterminating species in the Sixth Great Extinction,
A sin of convenience, this black mark of distinction.

Climate change spreads wider the brooding cloud of guilt
As earth burns feverish in full global wilt.
Ignoring the signs, we pray to technology,
Our techno-divinity, a manmade theology.
Sins of convenience are universally committed.
At the cost of moral injury, from which none is omitted.

STRIVING FOR ZEROS

Capitalism cultivates ambitious meritocracy,
Governed by a power-hungry, egoistic plutocracy
Where special interests manipulate democracy
In order to perpetuate entrenched aristocracy.

Where material wealth is the reward for merit,
And few are the wealthy who'll readily share it.
How can it be that the wealthy don't care at
All that greed punishes those who must bear it?

The higher reach of the soul and spirit
Is the domain of saints who strive to come near it,
Whose wisdom is lost on those who don't hear it.
The ideal is in reach, but many still fear it.

The future should reflect collective decisions,
But without common values we instead fuel divisions.
Mankind is in need of soulful revisions
To mandate equity in global provisions.

Yet those who, feckless, acquire more zeros
Are widely revered as cultural heroes.
Fiddling in their castles, these errant neo-Neros,
Watch the world burn as they add up more zeros.

A SYMBIOSIS OF FINE MINDS

It was there I met the legend Stephen Hawking
Where a clot of people was standing around, talking.
Strapped to his wheelchair in the shade of aspen trees,
It was a warm day in Aspen with just the hint of a breeze.

I braked my bike and leaned it against a fence rail.
How strange he looked, so twisted up and frail.
Boldly I approached, and I saw him looking at me.
His face was contorted and pained, all could see.

I introduced myself and made it quite brief.
I touched his gnarled hand and perhaps saw his relief
That I didn't steep him in patronizing praise,
But man-to-man, eye-to-eye, met his curious gaze.

It was there I also met Hans Bethe, the famed
Manhattan Project architect, for the atoms he tamed.
I interviewed Bethe for an Aspen Times feature,
As he debunked "Star Wars" like a hell-fire preacher.

I was a poor student of physics and science,
And yet with Bethe made an easy alliance
In our shared liberal, political cause
Inveighing against Reagan's astrophysical flaws

It was there I pondered the wonder of dark matter,
Thanks to friend Nick DeWolf, Aspen's eccentric mad-hatter,
Who brought me into his physics fold with chortling laughter,
A renegade outlier who I remember long after.

With Maggie, his wife, they threw lavish parties
The guests were no dunces, most of them smarties.
Nick's computer programmed the Hyman Mall fountain.
Through each random pattern one can see Aspen Mountain.

Nick, whose blond locks draped down his back,
Nick, who a fatal cancer would later attack,
Nick, who fought back and with death did vie,
Nick, who vowed, "I'll show them all how to die!"

Even when there was no specific assignment,
I would drop in to breathe an air of refinement,
Where quarky physicists find esoteric reward
With enigmatic equations chalked upon their blackboard.

RUMINATIONS

And if your faith in us endures,
We'll sing you hymns and songs.

SUNRISE ON MT. SOPRIS FROM ST. BENEDICT'S MONASTERY
SNOWMASS, COLORADO

HE'S HER MAN

The car door makes a muffled thump.
She hears his footsteps on the stairs
His coming gives her throat a lump
For the disappointments that she bears.

The clock blinks 3:00 in numbers red.
He closed the bar again.
Or found someone to take to bed.
Please no, dear God, amen.

The waiting wife, she plays the part,
The TV to console her.
A glass of wine, that's just the start,
White wine just makes her colder.

Now he's home, she's feigning sleep,
But tracking every motion.
The price she's paid for love ain't cheap.
Her tears could fill an ocean.

How often he has betrayed her trust,
A victim of temptation.
How quickly he has given in to lust,
Without recrimination.

She hears the working of his hands
Unclasp the big belt buckle.
They both wear sacred golden bands.
Hers chafes on her fourth knuckle.

She hears him sigh, slip in beside,
Smells whiskey, cigarettes.
There's no one for her to confide,
Lamenting her regrets.

Another night, how many more?
How long can she deny?
It's no use even keeping score.
Another night to cry.

The morning brings the light of day.
He wakes and she's not there.
He groans, rolls over, naught to say.
He couldn't really care.

The smell of coffee, crisping bacon,
The clatter of a pan.
The bond once held is long forsaken
T'ween woman and her man.

CONTACT!

Contact! Preached Henry D. Thoreau.
By god, the man ought to know,
Communing with the universe at Walden.

Touching only what is real,
Embracing all that one can feel
Finding union with pure matter.

So, go throw your cell phone in the lake,
To value the real and never the fake
And sense the vital world alone.

No need for prompts to make reply
To call hello or bid good-bye.
Choose your words, know what to say.

Demand the truth and not the fiction,
Rub up against and feel the friction
Of your living, pulsing being.

Go on now, try it, ignore your devices.
Realize just what the price is
Of techno-isolation.

We are made to feel and touch.
Let's go beyond and see how much
Life can bring in every moment.

The world is beautiful right out there,
So breathe in deep and taste the air
In true, unfiltered connection.

MYSTERY

All questions we pose are not to be answered,
No matter the ponderous head-scratching quest.
Intuitive knowing may hang on a chance word
Spurring ideas one might never have guessed.

Mystery, for science, is something to banish.
Ignorance, for modern man, is a sin.
Innocence is an affront that must vanish.
The prison of logic our minds trapped within.

Introspection is the loss of our age.
The realm of more curious minds.
Mystery is what nurtures the sage
And awakens the soul to the wonders it finds.

COSMIC RIDDLE

When pondering a celestial plan
Consider how snowflakes fall.
Drifting any which way they can
On a breeze, a gust, or a squall.

The riotous tumbling flakes I watch
Beyond my frosted windowpane
While sipping a dram of my favorite scotch
I wonder how one can ascertain

Faith in order, intelligent design,
Controlling the uncertainties of life.
Snowflakes incontrovertibly define
How random is pleasure and strife.

How could there be celestial guidance
Given chaos in a winter storm?
The laws of man are a mere contrivance,
Inapplicable to nature's free form.

Did the Big Bang spawn intelligent matter?
Or is randomness the cosmic MO?
I ponder as I climb my ladder
To clear my eaves of drifted snow.

Deposited there without instruction,
Nothing told it how to fall.
Nor the complex crystalline construction,
Which man cannot predict at all.

Great forces at work, beyond all reason,
The laws of physics give us pause.
The intellect is overthrown by treason
When we fail to grasp the deepest cause.

As much as we think we can predict
We can only know but a little.
And what we know may contradict
The ultimate cosmic riddle.

Watch the snow fall helter-skelter.
Feel it tickle on your cheek.
Feel the cosmos in its welter.
Man has every reason to feel meek.

What determines how the snow falls?
Flakes tumble down in every direction.
Their random pattern surely recalls
A wild, chaotic insurrection.

'THANK YOU FOR YOUR SERVICE'

The uniform was my shield, to keep me from all harm.
The weapon that I carried became an extension of my arm.
I was highly trained to kill, to take on any foe.
There was just one fatal weakness that I didn't even know.

When I killed and watched him die, his blood was on my hands.
Conscience bound my heart within constrictive iron bands.
Now the uniform is gone, my weapon's turned to rust,
And the reasons that I fought are covered in the dust.

I was a desert warrior, brave and strong and proud.
Now I'm just a nameless man, lost among the crowd.
There's no pill to heal my wounds, nothing kills the pain.
My life is hanging by a thread, it's swirling down the drain.

So, fly your flags and say the pledge—they don't mean jack to me.
My heart is torn, my soul is dead, so save your sympathy.
Don't thank me for my service; hell, I was just a kid.
You'll never know the things I saw or know the things I did.

The truth of moral injury is it outlives any crime,
So, I'm floating here in limbo, livin' on borrowed time.
My finger's on the trigger now, but there's no enemy
Other than my haunted self, my sights are set on me.

IN THE MIRROR

In the mirror, a reverse reflection.
I see myself from the wrong direction.
It's all backwards, turned around.
I see myself, but doubts abound.

I raise my left arm, but see my right.
Is there something wrong with my sight?
Of the truth, I'm confused, bereft.
I raise my right, and up goes my left.

It looks like me, that's my perception.
Is it so, or a reverse deception?
It's me all right, a like composite
But it's not me; it's my opposite.

FIFTY YEARS AFTER

She said our love was not to last,
That she'd forget, and so would I.
For what is lost, far in the past,
We'll laugh when looking back, or cry.

But fifty years, and I'm still longing
For the sparkle in her eyes.
To her my heart is still belonging.
After fifty years, I realize

That time cannot erase what was real.
First love makes forever changes.
Time cannot erase what you feel,
First love forever rearranges.

Looking back, I see her clearly.
Our lives apart don't reconcile.
Back then, we loved each other dearly.
My first love still makes me smile.

BREAD

Bread should be worthy to chew.
A bite should require a toothy tug.
Good bread is requisite with stew.
For a panophile, the ultimate drug.

About bread, let's be specific:
It must have texture as well as flavor.
Shun the processed bread, how horrific:
Soft, sans character and savor.

Bread should be heavy, solid, firm,
And, oh, how crucial is the crust.
Bread should please the palate and confirm
That in flour, salt and water one can trust.

But don't forget a critical ingredient
That gives bread leaven for any feast.
No baker should lack that small expedient,
The fermented blessing that's found in yeast.

Without this rising, formative influence,
Bread is stiff and flat and low.
When ingredients are in confluence,
A perfect loaf is worth the dough.

WORK GLOVES

New, they're stiff and wanting wear,
Good for pulling thistle stalks.
Oiled, they give the hands soft care,
Right for shoveling snow from walks.

Mine feel best on hickory ax handles,
Swinging home the double bit.
Please don't do that wearing sandals.
That could hurt, and quite a bit.

Old and used, they fit your hands,
Form to contours, know your grip.
Do whatever chore demands,
Trusting they will never slip.

Work without them and feel the malice
Of blisters as they swell and burst.
It takes a while to grow a callus.
Best to wear your work gloves first.

CAMPFIRE

Flickering campfire on a windless night,
A peaceful, cozy setting.
As smoke rises up beyond the light,
Thoughts of travail I'm forgetting.

A fire for cooking is all about coals.
Clean heat is what you're needing.
Boiling water is the first of your goals
In preparing Ramen for the eating.

Then heap on the wood for scotch and a smoke
And stories to share with friends
Of campsites past, with a satisfying toke
As with embers the dimming day ends.

STORM SCARE

The barometric pressure falls.
I watch with anticipation
As a snowstorm with a long duration
Brings a drama that recalls

A morning sky, so dim and dark,
With pallor gray the sun was muted.
The flakes drifted in all convoluted
And flocked the trees in nearby park.

Their branches were all stripped and bare,
The storm did not them bother,
As a child, I once observed my father
Ignore a storm without a care.

A blizzard closed both schools and roads.
A little boy, I filled with fear.
The world seemed menacing and drear.
My dad assured our roof would hold.

A home is sweetest when it's storming
When wind will batter at the sill.
I gazed from windows' frosted, chill
To witness snowdrifts quickly forming.

Now a father, I must calm the minds
Of children who think storms a fright,
And ease them through a windswept night
To wake and see what morning finds.

A bright new world that soon awakes,
The park across the street remade.
Mantled 'neath a blanket laid,
White quilt of blizzarding flakes.

Hats and jackets, boots and gloves,
We hurry into winter clothes.
A whitened world with rosy nose,
We frolic in what childhood loves.

RANDY'S BEAR CLAW TOTEM

His bear claw necklace was more than show.
It protected its wearer from cascades of snow.
Don't need no beacons on the ski trail,
Just a bear claw necklace for this alpha male.

Where one ursine claw would seem to suffice
A second claw comes in handy against head lice,
And colds and flues and perhaps the mumps,
And blotchy skin and unsightly lumps.

A third claw shields what mountaineers find frightening:
The thunderous flash of deadly lightning.
When exploring untrod mountain ridges,
A bear claw charms those lofty hermitages.

A fourth claw guarantees a life of enjoyment.
It even protects its wearer from unemployment.
It hones perspective, from womb to tomb,
Allaying morbid fears of doom and gloom.

The fifth claw is the one that really matters.
For the wearer to walk beneath life's many ladders.
It protects sore knees and high blood pressure, alike;
It guards against flat tires while riding a bike.

It makes life cheery, the world harmonious.
It diverts temptations from things felonious.
This charm is strong, but this clause, beware:
It wasn't so lucky for the ill-fated bear.

IT'S ALL THERE ON THE SCREEN

Examining life through the screen,
The world is such a dreadful place.
It's all shown there, on the screen,
How tragic is the human race.

The world is viewed in technicolor.
Death and violence are the norm.
Without the screen we'd be much duller,
Media tantalizes every form.

All amped up by thrilling drama,
That's what it takes to entertain.
Nothing sells without the trauma.
Shock and horror the refrain.

The news you see is dark and dire.
Serials are raw, explicit.
Fear and dread take ratings higher.
Sensation knows no deficit.

Ad sales make it all go 'round.
Revenue's what it's all about.
A hundred channels can be found,
Which everyone can do without.

FORGIVE US

Forgive us, Father, we don't know
The harm that we have done.
The toll is great down here, below
Take it from your only son.

How could you know it, on Day Six,
That man would turn against you?
And now it's way too late to fix
The mess we've put you into.

Forgive us, Father, for the ways
We've learned to kill each other.
Forgive us, Father, for the days
We sacrificed our brother.

Forgive us, Father, we beseech,
Do not rain down your vengeance.
We think we maybe still can reach
Celestial transcendence.

Forgive us, Father, as we err,
After all, that's only human.
And even though you're in despair,
You must offer us some room in

That great big Godly heart of yours
To forgive our many wrongs.
And if your faith in us endures,
We'll sing you hymns and songs.

CIGARS FOR WOMEN

It used to be that cigars were just for men.
With port or single-malt in the cloistered den.
A fat cigar's what men would smoke
And tell a chauvinistic joke.

Today, cigars are just a trend,
Which to the purist must offend.
The nouveau puffer is a pretender,
Especially with the other gender.

Feminist women have come to grips
With something long and hard and hot between their lips.
A good cigar becomes a tobacco-laden phallus,
They puff them to the quick with joyful malice.

When they snip the tip off a nice imported blunt,
Any man will cross his legs in front.
Like unlucky Bobbitt, who's sorely lacking.
One snip and men will soon be packing.

Most cigar men simply must implore:
No woman's hand should touch the humidor.
That sacred chalice, the home of choice Habanas.
Must be kept off limits to any prima donnas.

But why should only men enjoy a choice Oscuro?
A woman's smoking pleasure is much more thorough.
A cigar is stronger than any average guy.
A stogie has the strength and size to satisfy.

A woman in a cigar bar is a big attraction.
The way she mouths it causes a reaction.
Men can't deny the feminine allure.
When a cigar woman's confidence is cocksure
.

Some prefer an eight-inch Churchill, big and firm.
Causing all the men around to squirm.
When women put a Cuban to the torch
Squeamish men feel they've been scorched.

The bulge there in your pocket sir, is that a Tiparello?
If that's a Robusto, sir, you are a lucky fellow!
How many men wish they were so endowed?
So they can stand up in a crowd.

OF WASTE AND WAR

To hate all waste is to hate all war
To know the cost of what's in store
To lose a pawn just to even the score
To suffer loss and the loss deplore
To give your all and to give no more
To lose a life and death abhor
To honor glory and glory adore
To hear the thunder of the canon roar
To bear the cost of unspeakable gore
To mourn the ghosts of the vanquished corps
To gaze and see beyond death's door
To fornicate with the martial whore
To drink and forget on Lethean shore
To hear the shouts of the oaths men swore
To fabricate heroes with fictive lore
To pare God's apple down to the core
To mourn what nothing can restore
To feel the weight the pallbearers bore
To beg forgiveness and God implore
To do again what's been done before

PEACE IN OUR TIME

Peace in our time
Was Chamberlin's fix.
Hitler had other plans.
Europe was broken,
Like pickup sticks:
Ozymandias buried in sands.

Peace is the fleeting
Hope of mankind,
The source of optimist schemes.
War is the default
That keeps defeating,
Vain idealistic dreams.

AUTUMN MORNING

Autumn morn in late September,
Frosted ground, I will remember.
Blue the sky; the sun so bright.
The quaint log cabin feels just right.

But this is more than mere contentment,
I'm elated by a joyous sentiment.
As the cook stove pops and crackles
I realize I've cast off my shackles.

My time is mine, nobody's business.
Cartesian thought describes my is-ness.
Free to plumb my ethereal soul,
The wonder of being my relished goal.

Soon I leave, to home return,
Pondering what did I learn:
To hit the pause and feed life's fire
Warmed with joy, a deep desire.

WINDFALL

To be born is not a choice.
One big push, and there you are.
A breath-giving slap helps find your voice.
The cosmos marks your guiding star.

My birthright was due to luck.
Of parents' genes a mix I am.
On mother's nipple, my first suck
Attached me to a loving dam.

My parents were ardent intellects,
Read books galore, attended plays.
Sought culture in artistic sects.
With artisanal displays.

High speech and all the great ideals
Provided liberal views.
Good cooking and gourmet meals,
French cuisine and savory stews,

Osmotically, it all sunk in;
Respighi, Bach and Mozart
Vivaldi, Wagner, Borodin
The Louvre, the Met and modern art.

I learned to speak with clever tongue,
My tenses right and good syntax.
Read English lit. when I was young,
Memorized disparate facts.

Assured a place in society,
Fit for circles of elites,
Acted with propriety,
Learned the ropes, how one competes.

And threw the whole damned game away,
Lost trust in the Establishment.
Entitlements I would defray
Eschewing excess blandishments.

A simple life I'm living now.
Ascetic? Not what I would say.
I'm free to do as I allow,
And live my truth in every way.

THE OLD MAN

Trees bend in the wind, but not the old man.
He planted his foot and took root in the land.

A stoic, he defiantly stood the test of time
With the stridence of a zealot innocent of a crime.

Not once did he yield to a contrary thought,
And with steadfast resolve, his own truths sought.

No argument swayed him, all evidence aside.
Empirical truths he vehemently denied.

Obstinate, contentious, belligerent, firm,
His reproofs were strident and made lesser men squirm.

His views were so rigid, his mien so severe,
That if ever you crossed him, he'd grin ear-to-ear.

He loved a strong argument and fared well on most,
And for that reputation, he had never need to boast.

Where his grounding came from, nobody knew.
He stuck to his guns, taking aim at what was true.

When his time finally came, when he took his last breath,
He lost his final argument with inarguable death.

REALIZATIONS

From on high, the ramparts call
With the crashing cascade of rock fall.

MOONLIGHT ON CAPITOL PEAK
MAROON BELLS-SNOWMASS WILDERNESS

PREHENSILE

Here's a truth about our stuff:
We can never get enough.
Stone Age tool to complex utensil,
We want it all; we're born prehensile.

With our fine opposable thumbs,
We're not some stupid ape-like bums
Living lives uncouth and rough.
Instead, we hunt and gather stuff.

Desperate for what's coming next,
FOMO keeps us tuned to text,
Sitting fat on fleshy bums
And working only with our thumbs.

ANOTHER DAY

Winds that blow in stormy autumn,
Twirling, twisting yellow leaves
That gather where the gusts have brought them,
Swirled in corners, stacked like sheaves.

So revolve the changing seasons
Mother Earth's celestial clock,
Ticking off the time by reason
Of this spinning ball of rock.

Third from out the sol we rotate
Round the everlasting sun.
Overhead, by stars, we locate
The vast ellipse where we've begun.

The winds of time blow hard and steady,
From past to future is one-way.
Round and round now, all is ready
To announce another day.

WHAT IS LOVE?

Undying desire
Insatiable longing
Deep affection
Joy of togetherness
Spiritual union
Electricity of touch
Magnetism of the eyes
Fixation on voice
Unflagging care
Natural poetry of words
Joining of two hearts
Ache of separation
Inner knowing
Self-sacrifice
Assurance
Timelessness
Reciprocity
Caring

THE ONE THAT GOT AWAY

I awake with a start when I hear it—slap!
From the kitchen corner where I'd set the trap.
In dread I hear the flop, flop, flop,
Praying that soon the flop will stop.
In time, blessed quiet comes to bear.
I sleep not, knowing a mouse is there.

Day dawns the next peaceful morning.
I enter the kitchen with a sense of warning.
Glancing at the pantry door,
I know what I am looking for.
There sits the trap; its jaws are sprung,
But no mouse is there, not a one.
The peanut butter's been licked clean,
But no cadaver's to be seen.

With empty trap, my mind's reposing.
No grim remains to be disposing.
Clever that Houdini mouse,
Free again to roam the house.
Relieved, I'm happy; that's okay.
I'm grateful this one got away.

GEOLOGY

From on high, the ramparts call
With the crashing cascade of rock fall.
Snowmelt loosens redrock crags.
Boulders roar down like raging stags.

Mountains can't forever stay,
All will crack to broken clay.
Humanity's grand schemes and plans
Leave ruins built with callused hands.

I have seen the Rockies crumble.
One day old Gibraltar will tumble.
All that stands must face decay.
So, will our love be here to stay?

WOE IS ME

I oft reflect to purge my woes,
Then discover I've none of those.
I have all of my fingers, all of my toes.
What more could I want, a restructured nose?

I must be an exception to a psychological rule.
Not to have woes? Why, I must be a fool.
When I share that with folks, the reception is cool.
"He's just in denial, for life is a gruel."

In this, forgive me, I must disappoint.
Not having woes; I thought that was the point.
That's why woeful people find themselves out of favor.
With the happy-go-lucky, who live with savor.

For happiness can't be as easy as that.
I must have aches. Isn't my belly too fat?
Not confessing woes makes me feel like a rat,
Which gives me woe, and I'm okay with that.

THE LIBERTARIAN

Why should I comply to your decree?
I don't owe nobody nothin'.
I live my life in the Land of the Free.
To Americans that must mean somethin'.

Your liberal agenda means nada to me.
You just want to steal my freedoms.
That's not my road to liberty,
I shun self-righteous kingdoms.

I'll do whatever I'm entitled to do,
And your social mores won't stop it.
Try making peace between Arab and Jew.
As to controlling my life, you can drop it.

It's not worth you trying to win over my mind
Using arguments dripping with morals.
My rebuttals are firm, my positions unkind
As I sit firmly on libertarian laurels.

You think you can change me, don't be pathetic,
And, if you force me, then beware!
Am I ignorant or just apathetic?
I don't know, and I sure as hell don't care.

ODE TO SIR WALTER RALEIGH

Now we hail Sir Walter Raleigh,
Though it seems like utter folly,
For historically he's one of our regrets.
'Cause this Englishman went wacko
For exporting tobacco,
And without him we might not have cigarettes.

Well, the Indians knew better
What to do about this bloke.
So they poisoned this go-getter
When they taught him how to smoke.

Little did you know, Sir Walter, when you set your sail,
That people would be dying for tobacco to inhale.
Your mission to America was prompted just by greed.
Now half a billion people are puffing on that weed.

You sailed from North America with riches for the Queen.
But little did she know that it was deadly nicotine.
It's not your explorations at which anyone could scoff,
But all you did was give the world a nagging smoker's cough.

Oh Walter, oh Walter Raleigh,
You gave us Winston, Lucky, Pall Mall, Salem.
Light 'em, smoke 'em and inhale 'em.
Walter, oh, Walter Raleigh,
The cigarette is hot, by golly, hotter than a hot tamale.

Your rivals brought home souvenirs, like spice from Tenerife,
But Walter, you dropped ashes when you smoked a rolled up leaf.
You claimed that on your voyage you were blessed with steady breeze,
And now there's emphysema, it's making smokers wheeze.

Now Walt, with all your royalty, they said that you'd go far.
To think that nowadays you're known for resins and for tar.
You were a social climber rising up on every rung.
That was before the cigarette was found to give black lung.

Oh, Walter, oh Walter Raleigh,
Now we've got Vantage, Dunhills, Kent and Merit.
Smoke 'em and your clothes will wear it.
Walter, oh Walter Raleigh,
The cigarette's a hit, by golly, selling like a hot tamale.

And now the Surgeon General warns us to beware:
That smoking is quite dangerous, it dirties up the air.
The big tobacco companies complain that isn't fair.
If not for their carcinogens, what good is Medicare?

Oh, Walter, oh Walter Raleigh,
We still have stogies, chewers and pipe puffers,
Smokeless cigarettes and snuffers.

Walter, oh Walter Raleigh,
The cigarette is hot, by golly, hotter than a hot tamale.

PHALLUS

Going against one's sexual desire
Can set a man's soul on fire.
It's contrary to Nature's plan;
A man is a man is a man is a man.

Psychologists cite the ways of Hermes;
Each man needs to spread his spermies.
He's not in charge, but only his phallus,
For Ruth and Beth and Julie and Alice.

A mythic satyr was Dionysius.
According to the mythologist's thesis.
His sensuality was fantastic.
His sole joy was to be orgiastic.

Society endorses monogamy,
Which cynics say leads to monotony.
The procreation gene will never rest,
No matter how much spouses may protest.

Betwixt male and female there's a big gap
That goes beyond each other's lap.
The erect phallus is in man's genetic makeup.
Boys sometimes have one when they wake up.

It starts with blastula, the XY chrom,
Then mix in some high test testosterone.
Soon you've got a real teste male,
Iron John, rattling the bars of his jail.

WELTSCHMERZ

Dissatisfaction and hopeless despair
Combine in potent emotion.
Enervated by life's sad commotion
Life can seem terribly unfair.

But then, who made any other promise?
Fulfillment, happiness, there's no guarantee.
We blunder in obedience to a divine decree
To suffer angst when life goes amiss.

Living, even well, most everyone suffers.
No matter how evolved, there is no hall pass.
We mire in the swamp of moral impasse.
The arts, conversation, good wine are the buffers.

Companions come and go, some with good cheer,
But in the end, we travel the dim road alone.
Lamenting existence with a shrug and a groan.
Atoning, our reddened eyes shed a tear.

Global sorrow comes from universal pain,
When peace and love are elusive.
The reason to be remains inconclusive.
Life's symphony decrescendos in somber refrain.

THE PITCHFORK

The pitchfork is the Devil's tool,
A prod for any hellish ghoul.
But in the garden, the tool's divine,
Tilling grapes that turn to wine.

Plunge it deep with weighted foot
To aerate the fecund root.
Lever up a wormy clod,
The raw material of earthly sod.

And so we interface with the soil,
Obeying the law of sinful toil
When man was cast from paradise
For what He saw with holy eyes.

To labor for our daily bread,
No easy bliss, but work instead.
The first green chutes, nature's sign of love,
Blest with rain from heaven above.

Man's seed was planted in Eve's sweet furrow,
Where a million tiny worms did burrow.
Life comes up to be consumed,
From sheaf of wheat or fertile womb.

The harvest is a time of birth,
From the fount of hallowed earth.
All must go back down again,
So, grip the pitchfork and, amen.

YOU'RE IN IT

You're in it alone when you're making the call
With no one to back you, no one at all.
It's the way that you see it that counts in the end.
When no one else sees it, you haven't a friend.

But you stick with your truth, thanks just the same.
You give it your all in life's vital game.
You rely on your soul without qualm or shame.
Some call that courage, just to give it a name.

You pay for your values, if you have any at all,
And you pay with your heart, and you pay standing tall.
So, what does it get you and those who will stand
For what they believe and what they demand?

There's cheer if you prove it, the course you did stay,
And there's fear if you lose it for all that you'll pay.
But stand true you must if you honor your life.
Regret is far worse than enduring in strife.

PAIN AND PLEASURE

The mind rules the body until pain
Rules the body and informs the brain
That though the mind wants to go,
The body insists that it go slow.

The hobbling gait can irritate
And frustrate a mind that hates to wait
For mobility in spite of lost agility.
Acceptance is the way to tranquility
Along the path to sustainability.

Pain can be measurable,
But rarely is it pleasurable.
Tolerance grows in form or fashion,
With painkillers that one must ration.
Some pain must to all befall
To old and young, to big and small.

ABBREVIATIONS

Billy finds himself aboard
The *Bellipotent* where he's adored.

BILLY BUDD
BY HERMAN MELVILLE

Billy Budd, an orphaned sprout
Not too smart, but mighty stout
Nature's true barbarian is
Much too pure to taint with sin

Billy's pressed from "Rights of Man,"
Or vice-versa, he waves his hand
Saying adios to shipmate friends
But this ain't where the story ends.

Billy finds himself aboard
The *Bellipotent* where he's adored.
Intrigues lead to questions/answers
Billy's warned by old hand Dansker.

Claggart wants to nip young Budd;
He drags his name through the mud.
When he accuses Billy unfairly
Billy's roundhouse decks him squarely

"Starry" Verre, the wistful captain,
Convenes a courtroom in his cabin.
Billy's plight is left to Verre;
His feet will dangle in midair.

The laws of nature are put aside
The laws of man, we must abide.
Mournful sailors watch Billy swing.
Justice is a complex thing.

Tragic though the story goes
It's hard to say who are the foes.
On deep conundrums we must stew
Melville says, "This Budd's for you."

WAR AND PEACE
BY LEO TOLSTOY

Cossacks, Hussars join the Russians,
Austrians, and even sometimes Prussians.
Fighting foes Napoleonic,
Led by the diminutive demonic.

Throughout intrigues and romances,
Lavish balls and swirling dances,
Sleigh rides, drunken escapades,
Feckless nobles promenade.

Flaunting their hypocrisy,
The Russian aristocracy
Woos and screws and breaks taboos.
While ugly battles bring bad news.

1812, tumultuous year,
Borodino made that clear.
Burned up their beloved Moscow.
Made them wish they had a Costco.

Then there comes a change of seasons,
One of only several reasons
For Napoleon's undoing
In the long retreat ensuing.

Facing frigid Russian winter,
Le Grand Armée begins to splinter.
Burdened down with stolen loot
They have no hands freed up to shoot.

Picked off slowly as they fled,
Soon le Grand Armée was dead.
Costly was the French retreat.
Napoleon was in defeat.

Somehow odd Pierre survives.
Changes roles and changes wives.
Gives up freedom for his spouse,
Who rules the roost and runs his house.

THE VISIT
A PLAY BY FRIEDRICH DÜRRENMATT

A German town of past renown
Where the townsfolk sure are down.
A billionairess arrives by train
To tarnish Alfred Ill's good name.

Alfred's teen-aged procreation
Ruined Clara's reputation.
She became a shameless whore,
Her husbands total nine or more.

Clara makes a stunning offer:
Kill Ill to fill Güllen's coffer.
Now the townsfolk all must choose.
Soon they're wearing yellow shoes.

They buy new cars and fancy things.
A dirge to Ill the choir sings.
Güllen's fate will be fulfilled,
So Ill resigns, he will be killed.

The town conspires behind his back.
Cause of death? Heart attack.
Though the Gülleners are rich,
Democracy is in the ditch.

VOCALIZATIONS

(The following musical satires are sung to well-known tunes.)

This is the story of a hut trip that went well beyond the norm,
When seven Front Range skiers went out into a storm.

THE PRE-DAWN START TO A HUT TRIP
ASHCROFT, COLORADO

THE DOWNVALLEY SHUFFLE
Standard blues progression—PAUL ANDERSEN

I do the downvalley shuffle.
I commute in my car.
Stop at Woody Creek and have a beer at the bar,
And then I shuffle (shuffle-shuffle).

I'm just a buzzing worker bee on this ribbon of death.
It's Killer 82 and you can hold your breath . . .
And do the shuffle.

I used to live upvalley, thought it really was great.
A flimsy old shack with twenty roommates,
But now I shuffle (shuffle-shuffle).

I drive a killer four-lane highway,
It's no wonder I'm glum.
First a trailer park in Rifle,
Now a Parachute slum.
Downvalley shuffle.

(Break)

I tried to ride the bus, but it wasn't so nice.
I'd rather take my chances on that deadly black ice,
And do the shuffle (shuffle-shuffle).

So if I'm up real early and I leave by five.
I stand a fifty-fifty chance of getting to work—alive,
Downvalley shuffle . . .
I do the shuffle . . .
The downvalley shuffle . . .

ACID RAIN
"A Summer Song"—CHAD & JEREMY

When acid rain
Burns right through my window pane,
I think about the plains in Spain,
They're dying, too.

Trees . . . swayin' in the summer breeze,
They're dyin' of a strange disease,
What can we do?

They say that all good things must end, someday.
All the trees must fall.
But don't you know, that the lakes will go
And fish and algae, too.

Can we ski on acid snow?
Oh, no, no, no.

So when the rain
Leaches in my water main,
I'll get that acid buzz again,
And I'll go too.
And you'll go too.
We'll all go, too.

FOUR AND TWENTY
"Four and Twenty Years Ago"—STEPHEN STILLS

Four and twenty years ago,
My head was full of hair.
Long, thick and flowing,
And now the damn thing's bare.

I'm so tired of being bald.
And I don't appreciate the names I'm called.
And I think I'll get some hair plugs installed.

A warning comes with sunrise,
To cover up my head.
Sunburn leaves blotches.
Melanoma is my dread.

I'm so tired of this doo,
But there ain't a helluva lot that I can do,
And it saves a lot of money on shampoo.

They tell me there's a treatment,
Don't cause you any pain.
Guess I'll soak my head
In a gallon of Rogaine.

I'll embrace a new sense of peace
When my head will once again become a masterpiece.
If Rogaine doesn't work, I'll get a new hair piece.

GARY AND DONNA
"Frankie and Johnny"—Traditional

Gary and Donna were lovers,
And lordy, how they did love.
She sat on his knee,
While on Bimini,
And called him her sweet turtledove.
She loved that man,
But she was doin' him wrong.

Gary was running for office.
A president, he could be.
Then Donna he wooed.
He really got screwed.
We saw the whole thing on TV.
She loved that man,
But she was doin' him wrong.

Donna was a pretty young model.
An innocent lass, so they say,
But his heart she stole,
With body and soul,
By modeling her lingerie.
She loved that man,
But she was doin' him wrong.

Gary was ripe for a scandal,
Constantly tailed by the press.
He said, "Come along,
I've done nothing wrong."
And sailed away on "Monkey Business."
She loved that man,
But she was doin' him wrong.

Now Donna is suddenly famous.
Her book will be out any day.
But Gary's a schmuck.
The guy's out of luck.
She must have been one hell of a lay.
She loved that man,
But she was doin' him wrong.

She loved that man,
And sold him out for a song . . .

GHOST BIKERS IN THE SKY
"Ghost Riders in the Sky"—STAN JONES,
Performed by Shifty Freewheel

A mountain biker pedaled out one dark and windy day.
Upon a ridge he smoked a joint, then went along his way.
When all at once a peloton of pedal-heads he saw
A ridin' down a single-track and up a cloudy draw.

    Ki-yay . . . Yippee-Yi-Ooooooooo
    Ghost bikers in the sky

Their wheels were true, their frames were light, titanium, I'd say.
Their forks were straight, their angles steep, a thirteen-inch chain stay.
They looked so rad and bitchin' as they hammered through the sky,
And they wore the latest lycra shorts, with bulging calves and thighs.

    Ki-yay . . . Yippee-Yi-Ooooooooo
    Ghost bikers in the sky

Their faces tan, their eyes were red, their bottles filled with MAX.
Their fanny packs were stuffed with food, they carried hackie sacks.
They're gonna ride forever on that range up in the sky,
Strung out on beer and endorphins, wish I could get that high.

    Ki-yay . . . Yippee-Yi-Ooooooooo
    Ghost bikers in the sky

As the riders stroked on by him each had anguish on his face.
They were pushing hard the big chain ring, Shimano Biopace.
They tipped their caps said "Adios, we'll see you 'round some day,"
Then they stood up on their pedals . . . and sprinted far away.

    Ki-yay . . . Yippee-Yi-Ooooooooo
    Ghost bikers in the sky
    Yippee-Yi-Ooooooooo (fade)

HANG DOWN YOUR HEAD, JOHN RUEDI
"Hang Down Your Head, Tom Dooley"—THE KINGSTON TRIO

Hang down your head, John Ruedi,
Hang down your head and cry.
Hang down your head, John Ruedi,
Your reservoir is running dry.

Your dam flooded out poor Ruedi.
The people had to all move out.
Now California's calling
Because of climate change and drought.

Hang down your head, John Ruedi,
Hang it down on your chest.
Hang down your head, John Ruedi,
Your water is flowing west.

Your reservoir fills in springtime
And drains mighty low by fall.
Now the damn thing's nearly empty
Because of the compact call.

Hang down your head, John Ruedi,
There's nothing here that can be done.
Hang down your head, John Ruedi.
Adjudications have been won.

HOW DO YOU SOLVE A PROBLEM LIKE GADDAFI?
"What Do You With a Problem Like Maria?"—The Sound of Music—
ROGERS and HAMMERSTEIN

How do you solve a problem like Gaddafi?
What do you do with a guy who thinks he's God?
How do you solve a problem like Gaddafi?
A potentate, an dictator, a clod.

How do you tell Gaddafi he's not wanted?
How do you tame the ego of a lord?

The only guy we know, tells NATO where to go,
A one-man fundamentalist terror show, oh,
How do you solve a problem like Gaddafi?
How do you make a despot want to go?

*   *   *   *   *

He's a man without a qualm.
He's more evil than Saddam.
He will shoot civilians if that is his whim.

His couture evokes dismay.
Wears a toga and beret.
Both his moustache and his beard could use a trim.

He's as rotten as can be.
He's the scourge of Lockerbie.
There's no freedom when you're underneath his thumb.

All his rule has been a crime.
He's not ready for prime time.
He's a tyrant. He's a villain. He's a bum.

*   *   *   *   *

Oh, how do you solve a problem like Gaddafi . . . ?
How do you get this dic-ta-tor to go?

LITTLE HYPERCAR
"GTO"—THE BEACH BOYS

Oh little hypercar,
You're really lookin' fine.
You got composites and a fuel cell,
An aeronomical design.
I'm gonna really tack it up now,
And she don't even whi-i-ine.

She's my high-tech,
Fuel efficient,
Dual drive,
Hypercar.

Ooo-Ooo, my little hypercar
Ooo-Ooo, my little hypercar
Ooo-Ooo, my little hypercar

Gonna save all my money
To buy a hypercar.
I'll even raid my children's college fund.
You know I'll go that far.
And if it takes all my savings,
Oh well, it's au revoir, oir-oir.

In my high-tech,
Fuel efficient,
Dual drive,
Hypercar.
(chorus)

And when I finally get one,
I'll drive my hypercar.
From Pomono out to Glendale,
If she'll get that far.
While I'm reducing air pollution,
I'll smoke a fat cigar, ar-ar.

Well she's the funniest-lookin' thing around.
But little buddy my emissions' down.
In my high-tech,
Fuel efficient,
Dual drive,
Hypercar.

IF I ONLY HAD A JOB
"If I Only Had a Brain"—The Wizard of Oz
—HAROLD ARLEN and YIP HARBURG
In honor of collaborator Tracey Wickland

I would wake up in the a.m.
The bills I'd surely pay 'em,
And face the teeming mob.
I'd be fit as a fiddle, and could solve any riddle if I only had a job.

My steps would be much free-er.
My me would be much me-er.
I wouldn't sigh or sob.
I would know my ambition isn't only phony wishin' if I only had a job.

Picture me in penury,
Feeling bitter and annoyed,
In a waiting line just for the unemployed.
My livelihood is so devoid.

I'd flip burgers by the hour
And wouldn't feel so dour,
Working like a slave.
I would do what they tell me,
I would even let them sell me,
If I only earned a wage.

THIS LAND AIN'T YOUR LAND
"This Land is Your Land"—WOODY GUTHRIE

This land was your land,
But now it's my land,
From the lowest desert,
To the highest highland,
From the old growth forests,
To Gulf Stream oil fields.
This land was made for industry.

As I was driving
That six-lane highway,
Got stuck in traffic
On a strip-malled byway.
I saw above me
A jet-filled skyway.
This land was made for industry.
This land ain't made for you or me.

DON'T FENCE ME OUT
"Don't Fence Me In"—COLE PORTER

Oh, give me land, lots of land under starry skies above,
Don't fence me out.
Let me drill every hill for the oil and gas I love,
Don't fence me out.
Let me file on a claim wherever I please.
For coal and gas and oil and even beetle-killed trees.
Open up the forests for the industries,
Don't fence me out

THE LEADER OF IRAQ
"Leader of the Pack"—the Shangri-Las. Produced as written on National Public Radio's All Things Considered *in the late '90s*

We know he's got a weapons store . . .

He's got the means of mass destruction.
You get the picture?
Yes, we see.
That's why we went for the Leader of Iraq.

He is so helpless, what can he do?
Saddam is scorned by Arab and Jew.
He's really feelin' low.
His only friends are the PLO.
He's in deep doo-doo,
The leader of Iraq.

Now George is always putting him down.
He lives in a bunker deep underground.
Now we don't trust Saddam.
We think he's got the bomb.
That's why we went for the leader of Iraq.

(spoken)
So we sent in a UN inspection team . . .
And they found some top secret documents . . .
And just as they were trying to get away
A bunch of Iraqi soldiers came and . . .
Look out! Look out! Look out!

Now George is fuming, he's really sore.
He may send our troops back into war.
Saddam ignored our words.
Instead, he wiped out the Kurds.
That's why we hate you,
The leader of Iraq

Gone . . . leader of Iraq . . . you've gone too far
Gone . . . leader of Iraq . . . you've gone too far
Gone . . . leader of Iraq . . . you've gone too far
Go-o-o-onnnnnnnnnne . . .

THE NIGHT THEY TORE DOWN LITTLE NELL
"The Night They Tore Old Dixie Down"—ROBBIE ROBERTSON

Lester Crown is my name, I'm a man of fortune and fame.
I came here to build Little Nell and tear down the old again.
It was in the summer of '85, the recession was just barely alive.
I could tell by the DOW that my stocks all fell.
It was a time I remember oh so well.

The night they tore down Little Nell,
And all the people were screamin'.
The night, they tore down Little Nell,
And it was all from my scheming.
They went - No, no, no, no, no, no . . .

Donald Trump is my name, and I fly on my own jet plane.
I bought out John Robert's claim to develop the Meadows again.
It was in the winter of '86, when this city boy came out to the sticks.
I could tell it was time to buy, not sell.
It was a time I remember oh so well.

The night they tore down Little Nell,
And all the wall were crumblin'.
The night they tore down Little Nell,
And all the locals were grumblin'.
They went, No, no, no, no . . .

Here with my wife and family, Ivana she says to me,
"Donald, quick come see, here comes Mohammed Hadid."
Young and brash, he was just a kid.
He should never have tried to match my bid.
But the project penciled and he got the dough,
And all I could say is: sell high and buy low!

The night they tore down Little Nell,
And all the people were screamin'.
The night they tore down Little Nell,
And I must'a been dreamin'.
They went, No, no, no, no, no . . .

Mohammed Hadid is my name, and I was after some capital gains.
I wanted a Ritz Hotel, and I've got a couple of cranes.
It was the summer of '91, the Ritz and the Meadows,
    they should'a been done.
I was having attacks of anxiety 'cause my lender
    was trying to renege on me.

The night they tore down Little Nell,
And all the people were bitchin'.
The night they tore down Little Nell,
I only wanna be rich 'n famous.
Yeah, yeah, yeah, yeah, yeah . . .

Sheik Il-Ibraham is my name,
And Mohammed became a royal pain.
I came here to build a hotel, and I've got a castle in Spain.
As long as you all keep buyin' oil,
I'll make sure construction workers will toil.
This grand hotel will make history,
So say, hello, to your new prosperity.

The night they tore down Little Nell,
It was a big, ugly mess.
The night they tore down Little Nell,
And it was all about progress.
Don't you know, know, know, know . . .

ROCKY MOUNTAIN BUY
"Rocky Mountain High"—*JOHN DENVER*
In honor of collaborator Tracey Wickland

He was bored in the summer of his 27th year.
Bought a condo in a place he'd never been before.
He left poverty behind him, but soon he was bored again.
Now he's buyin' up the keys to every door.

When he first came to the mountains, he didn't really see,
All the money that was waiting to be made.
But then his eyes were opened to the values that are real,
Real estate, that is, his brand new stock and trade.

And it's a Colorado Rocky Mountain buy.
You can see it rainin' dollars from the sky.
Know he'd be a poor man if he didn't buy low sell high.
Rocky Mountain buy, Colorado
Rocky Mountain buy, Colorado

Well, he climbed the social ladder, he found rich investors there.
He saw dollar signs as far as he could see.
And they say that he got crazy once, and he tried to buy the sun,
'Cause he heard that solar power was the key.

Now he walks in quiet wonder, the forests and the streams,
Buying land with every step he takes.
And his sight has turned inside himself as he tries and understand
How to keep from paying the tax on what he makes.

And it's a Colorado Rocky Mountain buy.
You can see it rainin' dollars from the sky.
It's better to speculate than never, next week they'll be twice as high.
Rocky Mountain buy, Colorado
Rocky Mountain buy, Colorado

Now his wallet's full of money, but his heart still knows some fear,
Of a simple thing he cannot understand.
The interest rates keep rising, so it's harder every year,
And he's only trying to live off of the land.

And it's a Colorado Rocky Mountain buy.
You can see it rainin' dollars from the sky.
Talk to any realtor you will hear the same reply.
Now's the time to buy, Colorado
Grab your piece of pie, in Colorado
Rocky Mountain buy, Colorado . . .

THE BALLAD OF TAMMY AND JIMMY
"Sweet Betsy from Pike"—JOHN STONE

Hear now the story of young Tammy Faye.
Who met the redeemer and went all the way.
With Christian cosmetics and good Jimmy B.
And a nation-wide hook-up on Christian TV.

Not one to cater to tawdry display,
A pure life of good works for young Tammy Faye.
On a heaven-sent mission the two did embark,
With a fleet of Rolls-Royce and a Christian theme park.

Send checks or your pledges, their viewers they'd tell,
Enhancing the cash flow to our dear PTL.
Their rich, faithful listeners they'd not deceive,
As long as the faithful were completely naïve.

It turned out Jim's sermons were all smoke and noise,
To cover his trysts with the young choir boys.
There was always a handful whose singing was weak,
But with Jim, they were well trained at turning the cheek.

It came as a shock when their plans went to Hell,
And their empire crumbled to Jerry Falwell.
Well of course there's a lesson, you guessed it, old sod:
Vengeance is sweet when you screw 'round with God!

THE LOST SKIERS

Gilligan's Island theme song—"A Three Hour Tour..."
—*SHERWOOD SCHWARTZ* and *GEORGE WYLE*

This is the story of a hut trip that went well beyond the norm,
When seven Front Range skiers went out into a storm.
They started up at Ashcroft, going to the Goodwin-Greene.
At the fateful trailhead was the last time they were seen.

The warning signs were obvious, the forecast didn't lie,
And adding to the danger, the avalanche risk was high.
The skiers were provisioned, they had Power Bars and gorp.
It's best to carry lots of food when skiing with Ken Torp.
(When skiing with Ken Torp...)

He was the fearless leader and he seemed so very sure.
"Just follow me," he told his group, on a three-hour tour.
(A three-hour tour...)

As they were nearing Taylor Pass, the blizzard really hit.
They spent the night all huddled up inside a snowy pit.
Next morning didn't looks so good, the skiers now were lost.
Fed up and cold Andrea Brett skied out with Richard Rost.
(Made tracks with Richard Rost...)

As Rost and Brett skied down the road to report the others' plight
Elliot Brown and the leader Torp skied off and out of sight.
They said they'd meet the others in the trees down by the creek.
By the time these two were rescued, they'd been gone about a week.

The three remaining skiers, the Dubins and their friend,
Skied through the storm together, until the bitter end.
(Until the bitter end...)

Brigitte Schlugar said that she was told to drop her pack.
Rob Dubin then commanded her to break a fresh ski track.
The three found shelter in the snow, they dug themselves a cave,
And Schlugar said she felt just like a "beaten Roman slave."
(A beaten Roman slave . . .)

Meanwhile the rescue parties were combing every hill,
And racking up a twenty-thousand-dollar rescue bill.
With snowmobiles and snowcats, Army choppers and with dogs,
The rescuers were wording a touching epilogue.
(A touching epilogue . . .)

And then the skiers all were found, to everyone's delight.
Now Elliot Brown . . . and Ken Torp, too . . . Rob Dubin and his wife,
Brigitte Schlugar and the rest can sell the movie rights.
(Can sell the movie rights . . .)

AVILUNG
"Aqualung"—JETHRO TULL

Sitting on a hut bench
Bragging 'bout your awesome powder turns,
With Avilung.

Skiin' down the avi chutes,
Floater skis and knee-high boots,
And Avilung.

An avalanche roars down the slope.
Avilung my only hope,
Hey, Avilung.

****

Avilung, my friend, you keep me safe while skiing.
You say that I can breathe beneath the snow.

Avilung, I hope you are my life insurance
My premiums are spent on blower snow.

****

Clamp that hose between your lips.
Take the air in tiny sips,
From Avilung.

Sucking on a clogged up hose.
Snow is packed in ears and nose,
And in Avilung

Dying in an icy tomb.
Too bad the warrantee expires soon,
On Avilung.

GOODWIN GREENE
"Bittergreen"—GORDON LIGHTFOOT

Up to the Goodwin-Greene he skied
The ridge above the town.
Snow was gently falling,
Soft as eider down.
The avi risk was low, so
He hadn't any fear.
Dreaming of a beer . . .

Goodwin-Greene, it called him,
At the break of dawn,
Built by Alfred Braun
Long ago.
Goodwin-Greene, it called him, twenty-five below,
A place he loved to go, far away.

So now he's at the Goodwin-Greene,
The stove is piping hot.
Looking through his food sack,
He sees what he forgot.
Gotta live on Ramen
For the next three days,
In a stoned out haze.

Goodwin-Greene, it called him,
At the break of dawn,
Built by Alfred Braun, long ago.
Goodwin-Greene, it called him,
Buried in the snow,
A place he loved to go, far away.

DOWNTOWN
"Downtown"—JACKIE TRENT and TONY HATCH,
Sung by Petula Clark

If you want danger there is no place much stranger
Than a place I know,
Downtown.

A place in the city filled with sorrow and pity
Where the life is low,
Downtown.

Just listen to the news reports, they're morbid and so thrilling.
Murders happen every day, you might witness a killing.
Hope it's not yours.

Just go where the fine arts thrive.
Take in a Classical concert, if you can survive
When you're

Downtown,
Where all the lights are bright
Downtown
You could get in a fight
Downtown
Just don't go there at night
Downtown ... Downtown ...

It's all so easy, you can really feel sleazy
At a porno show,
Downtown

Where nothing suffices like fulfilling your vices.
Bring a lot of dough,
Downtown.

And if you drive in traffic where the cars are all polluting,
You may find excitement in a random drive-by shooting.
Bring your own gun.

So if you are going there, you'd better update your will
'Cause you won't have a prayer when you're

Downtown
Better to pass it by.
Downtown
Look no one in the eye.
Downtown
Hopefully you won't die
Downtown . . . Downtown . . . Downtown . . .

THE WRITER
"The Boxer"—PAUL SIMON

I am just a poor boy,
And a writer by my trade,
And I carry the rejections
Of everything that's been turned down,
By publishers and agents,
Who I thoroughly disdain.
How I hate them,
How I hate them,
They are driving me insane . . .

Why should I
Try to write such glowing prose?
Just so I
Can become a writer everybody knows?

Well, I used to write for pleasure,
To express my deepest need.
Now I pander to my clients,
Their enormous egos how I feed
With pandering and compliments,
There's no limit to my need.

How I hate them,
How I hate them,
How much can a writer bleed?

Lies and lies,
That's all that I can say.
Lies and lies,
That's the only way I'll earn my meager pay.

BOOKS BY PAUL ANDERSEN

In Search of Community

The Town that Said 'Hell, No!'

The Friends' Hut

High Road to Aspen

The Story of Snowmass

Moonlight Over Pearl

Aspen | Rocky Mountain Paradise

Aspen's Rugged Splendor

Power in the Mountains

East of Aspen

Aspen | Body, Mind, & Spirit

Elk Mountains Odyssey

The Preacher and the Pilot

Aspen | Portrait of a Rocky Mountain Town

Aspen in Color

ABOUT THE AUTHOR

PAUL ANDERSEN has been a professional writer for more than forty-five years.

His writing has earned him credits as a television scriptwriter, book author, screen writer, historian, magazine contributor, and columnist and contributing editor for the *Aspen Times*. He wrote a weekly opinion column, *Fair Game*, for over 30 years, for which he has won awards from the Colorado Press Association, and he is one of the longest continually published writers in the history of the *Aspen Times* over the course of four decades.

Andersen has published hundreds of newspaper articles, magazine features, authored fifteen books, written dozens of television scripts, and co-wrote the screen story for *China: The Panda Adventure* for IMAX Films (2000). His book, *High Road to Aspen*, written in collaboration with photographer David Hiser, won the Colorado Book Award's Gold Medal in June 2015.

Andersen's journalistic career began in 1977 as reporter for the *Gunnison Country Times*. In 1980, he became a reporter/editor for the *Crested Butte Chronicle*, where he reported on all aspects of Gunnison County. In 1984, he joined the editorial staff of the *Aspen Times* and covered Aspen thoroughly and joyfully.

In 2005, Andersen partnered with the Aspen Institute to create *Nature & Society*, an executive seminar that immersed participants in wilderness while exploring philosophical, literary and historical perspectives on man and nature.

In 2013, Andersen founded the non-profit Huts For Vets, which he designed to help US military veterans plagued by trauma and other psychological challenges find peace and healing in the wilderness at the 10th Mountain Huts of Aspen.

Today, Andersen leads wilderness hikes for the Aspen Institute where he moderates the Great Books seminars. He enjoys reading philosophy and literature, and he hikes, skis and bikes the mountains and deserts of the American West. Bicycle tours have led him across Europe and Eurasia.

Andersen lives outside Basalt, up the Frying Pan Valley, 25 miles from Aspen, with his psychotherapist wife, Lu Krueger-Andersen. Their 30-year-old son, Tait, lives in Basalt with his wife Sarah and their baby boy, Axel Andersen, named for Paul's Danish immigrant grandfather.

www.ingramcontent.com/pod-product-compliance
Lightning Source LLC
Chambersburg PA
CBHW020544030426
42337CB00013B/973